WHAT HAPPENS WHEN

Someone I love has Cancer

SECOND EDITION

written + illustrated by
SARA OLSHER

mighty -AND- bright™

helping families handle hard things

Hi, my name is Mia!

And this is Stuart.
Stuart feels better when he knows
what's going to happen every day.

(Actually, *everybody* feels better when they know
what's going to happen—even grown-ups!)

Most of the time,
we do the same things in the mornings.
We wake up.

We eat breakfast.
(I like apples. Stuart only eats bugs.)

Usually our nights are the same too.
We brush our teeth.

We put on our jammies, and we go to bed.
Every day ends with sleep.

But our days can be different.

Some days we go to school,
and some days are the weekend!

When something big changes,
what we do each day can change too.
Stuart wants to know what happens to our days
when someone we love has **cancer**.

But he doesn't really understand what cancer is. Do you?
Cancer is sort of like a sickness,
but you can't catch it like you catch a cold.

Here's how it works!

Every living thing is made up of tiny little guys called **cells**.

Cells are like blocks, but they put *themselves* together.
One really cool thing about cells is that one cell can
turn itself into two cells anytime it wants.
(*Whoa*, right?)

That means cells can build and build and build.
It's like building with LEGO™ and *never* running out of blocks!

imagine the tower you could build!

Every cell has a job.
Together they build body parts, then tell them how to work.
They make hearts pump, legs walk, lungs breathe,
and so much more!

Cells are very polite.
They give each other space to work,
and they stop making new cells when they have enough to do a job.

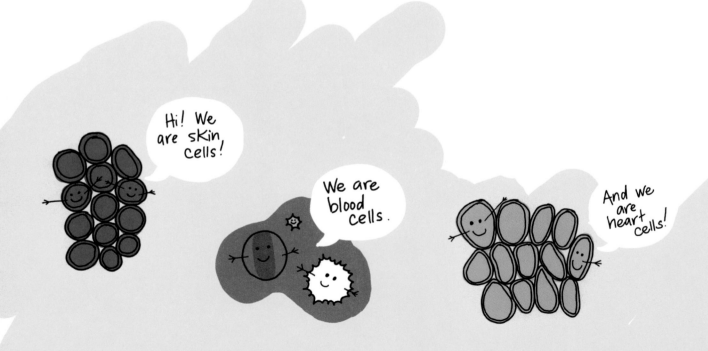

But sometimes a broken cell gets made.
It looks weird, acts weird, and doesn't know what its job is.
The only thing it remembers how to do is make more cells.

Nobody caused this cell to break.
It wasn't anything the person ate or did wrong! Sometimes cells break.

And one or two broken cells is no big deal,
because our healthy cells can get rid of them.
But sometimes the healthy cells don't see the broken cells ...

... and the broken cells keep making
more and more broken cells, faster and faster.

Before long, it's a *huge* mess.
This huge mess of broken cells is called cancer.

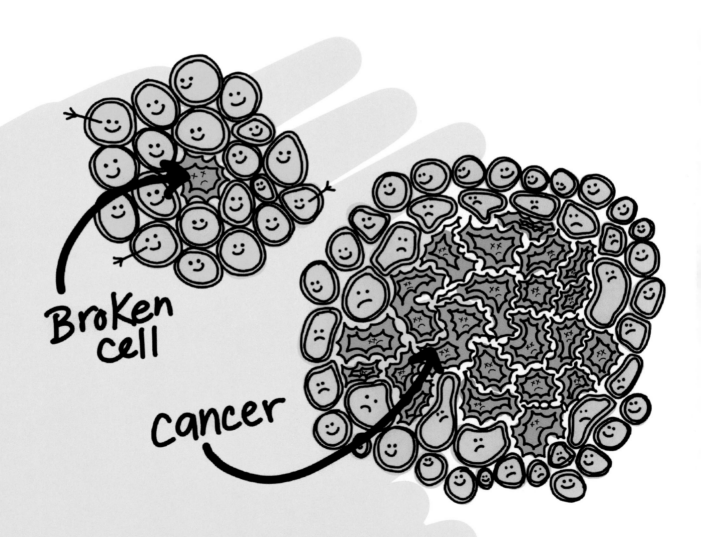

Broken
cell

cancer

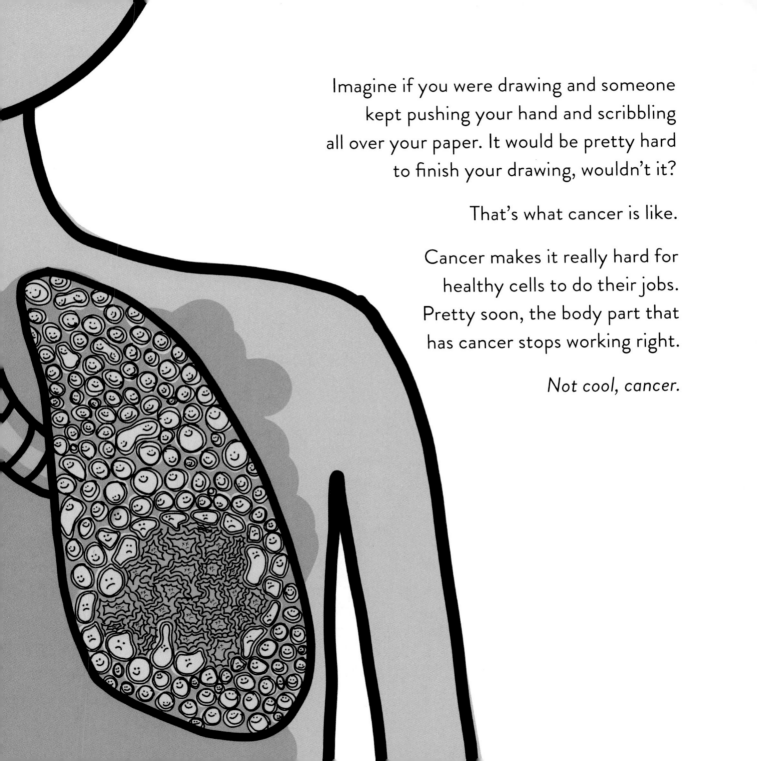

Imagine if you were drawing and someone kept pushing your hand and scribbling all over your paper. It would be pretty hard to finish your drawing, wouldn't it?

That's what cancer is like.

Cancer makes it really hard for healthy cells to do their jobs. Pretty soon, the body part that has cancer stops working right.

Not cool, cancer.

When our healthy cells get crowded by cancer,
they aren't able to do their jobs.
And if they can't do their jobs, our bodies might not work right.

So when someone finds cancer in their body,
they definitely want to get it out.

But how
do we get
cancer
out?

To get the cancer out, sometimes a
doctor will give someone surgery.

This means the doctors will make the person
go to sleep at the hospital, then carefully
take out the broken cells with a tiny knife.
The person doesn't feel anything.

This might mean the person isn't home for a
few days, because they are at the hospital.

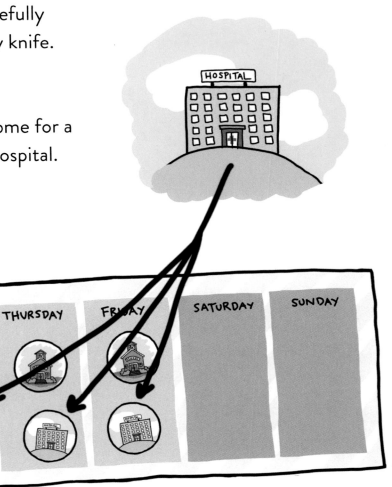

Sometimes, the doctors use a big machine to zap the cancer cells with a heat ray called radiation, and they all go away.

To get radiation, the person lays on a table while a machine sends out the rays. The person will go to the doctor for radiation every day (except the weekends) for many weeks.

Radiation doesn't hurt, but the person's skin might turn red, like a sunburn, and they also might get tired.

Both of these things go away pretty quickly after radiation is over.

Oh well, it won't last forever...

Doctors can also give the person medicine called chemo. The chemo medicine gets rid of the cancer, but it also does some very not-fun things.

One thing it does is kind of weird and maybe funny and also sad: It can make the person's hair fall out, so they are totally bald until they are done with chemo.

It also makes the person feel tired or sick for a long time. They can't run, jump, or play like they're used to.

To get chemo, the person goes to a special doctor appointment and sits in a chair for a few hours while medicine goes in their body.

Sometimes they go every week, and sometimes they go every few weeks.

Either way, they usually get chemo for months.

All this makes Stuart a little nervous.
He wants to know - what about me?
What's going to happen?

On some days, the medicine doesn't bother the person very much.
You can walk together, or drive places together.
There are a lot of activitites to look forward to.

But other days, the person's body might hurt or feel tired.
On those days, the person might need to do quiet activities,
like watch a movie — or they might just need to sleep.

Sometimes this is scary for kids. You are used to seeing the person strong
and active! Chemo makes their body feel weak, but inside
they are still strong — just tired.

People with cancer usually
know the days they
won't be feeling
well, so you can
plan activities around
how they're feeling.

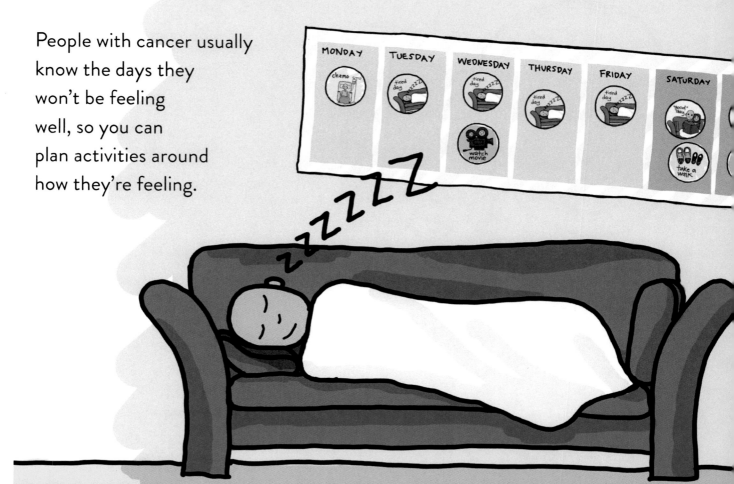

Sometimes their tiredness might make you sad or worried. It's okay to miss how things used to be! Unfortunately, there's nothing you can do to make cancer go away yourself. You didn't make it happen (that's impossible), and you can't stop it either.

Sometimes cancer means having different people dropping you off or picking you up at school, or being quiet while the person with cancer sleeps. That isn't fun, but when you know what to expect, it isn't scary either.

Some people have a cancer that will go away forever.
They can stop taking all or most medicines and just go for check-ups.

And some people will have cancer for the rest of their life.
They will need to take medicine or have treatments to try to keep the
cancer from making more broken cells.

When someone has cancer for the rest of their life, there might be times where they feel tired, and there are lots of times where they'll feel pretty good! They might even get their hair back.

Either way, the person will go for doctor check-ups to make sure the medicine is working, and they'll always let you know what the doctor says.

Stuart feels a lot better now that he knows what to expect.
Even though our days can be different, it helps to plan out our
week together so we know what's going to happen next.

We can give ourselves activities to look forward to, like making crafts,
watching a movie, or going to a friend's house to play.

And remember, it's important to share how you are feeling with a grown-up. All these changes can be hard! By planning special time together, you have a time when you know it's okay to talk about your feelings.

We can do hard things, together!

And don't forget, Stuart... even the biggest feelings don't last forever.

Hi! My name is Sara, and I had cancer, too.

I wrote this book (and 6 others!) because I like to draw + help people.

reading

Dancing (Badly)

my family

Things I LOVE!

nature

our dog, Honey

candy

Rainbows

Quiet time

(for awhile I didn't have any hair. I think my head is a lovely shape.)

I live with my daughter, my partner, his daughter, and our dog. I want a goat, and I want to name him CAULIFLOWER!

I do all my drawings on an iPad with an Apple pencil

Knowing what to expect makes cancer way easier.

(actually life is __always__ easier when you know what happens next!)

understand how they might be feeling!

know where they'll be + when

know who will drop you off + pick you up at school.

get excited for fun stuff!

find them at mightyandbright.com!

(along with loads of other helpful stuff!)

mighty ᴬᴺᴰ bright™

helping families handle hard things

Published by Mighty + Bright
mightyandbright.com

ISBN: 978-0578571386

Medical Disclaimer:
This book is not intended as a substitute for the medical advice of physicians.
The reader should regularly consult a physician in matters relating to his/her health and
particularly with respect to any symptoms that may require diagnosis or medical
attention.

Want to tell me something?
send a letter!
mia
c/o mighty + bright
555 5th Street #300F
Santa Rosa CA 95401

Made in the USA
Monee, IL
28 December 2021

87427842R00021